North America Butterflies

North America's Favorite
Butterflies

A Pictorial Guide

by Patti and Milt Putnam

WILLOW CREEK PRESS

MINOCQUA, WISCONSIN

PHOTOGRAPHY CREDITS
All photography by Milt and Patti Putnam except: Jaret C. Daniels, pages 9, 48, 49, 52, 53, 76 (top), and 117; Photo/Nats (Gregory Crisci, page 12), (Jeff March, pages 20 and 85), and (Steven Baglione, page 123); Elton N. Woodbury, pages 14, 25, 37, 46, 47, 58, 59, 66, 71, 78, 82 (top), 83, 89, 90, 91, 96, 98, 102, 110, 119, and 126; Leroy Simon, pages 19, 55, 93, 95, 113, and 124; Whit Bronaugh, page 18; Robert Campbell, pages 21, 24, 38, 41, 100, and 116; Thomas C. Boyden, pages 22, 31, 44, and 45; Visuals Unlimited (Leroy Simon, pages 26 top and bottom); John Shaw, pages 27, 30, 56, 60, 61, 62, 64 (top), 68, 72, 82 (bottom), 84, 94 (top and bottom), 107, 109, and 111; Larry West, pages 32, 43, 65, 67, 88 (top), and 97; Edward S. Ross, pages 40, 42, 81, 86, 87, 92 (all), 101, 112 (top and bottom), 114, and 115; Kerri Schwarz, page 63; Robert McCaw, pages 64 (bottom), 103, and 106; David Liebman, pages 70, 80, 88 (bottom), and 108; Unicorn Stock Photos (Ed Harp, page 99); Andrei Sourakov, pages 118 and 122; and Richard Day, page 120.

Published by Willow Creek Press, P.O. Box 147, Minocqua, Wisconsin 54548
For information on other Willow Creek titles, call 1-800-850-WILD

Design: Heather M. McElwain

Library of Congress Cataloging-in-Publication Data

Putnam, Patti and Milt.
  North America's favorite butterflies : a pictorial guide / by Patti and Milt Putnam.
    p.   cm.
  ISBN 1-57223-109-2
  1. Butterflies--North America--Identification. 2. Butterflies--North America--Pictorial works. I. Title.
  QL548.P88   1997
  595.78'9'097--dc21   97-9334
                                                                          CIP

Printed in Canada

TABLE OF CONTENTS

DEDICATION   8
    Schaus' Swallowtail 9

INTRODUCTION — *Butterfly Magic*   **10**

SKIPPERS   13
    Silver-spotted Skipper 14
    Long-tailed Skipper 16
    Checkered Skipper 18
    Fiery Skipper 20

SWALLOWTAILS   23
    Pipe-vine Swallowtail 24
    Zebra Swallowtail 26
    Black Swallowtail 28
    Anise Swallowtail 30
    Giant Swallowtail 32
    Tiger Swallowtail 34
    Spicebush Swallowtail 36

WHITE / SULPHURS   39
    Checkered White 40
    Cabbage Butterfly 42
    Sara Orange Tip 44

Alfalfa Butterfly 46
Dog Face 48
Cloudless Sulphur 50
Barred Yellow 52
Sleepy Orange 54

GOSSAMER WINGS 57
Little Copper 58
Purplish Copper 60
Gray Hairstreak 62
Eastern Tailed Blue 64
Spring Azure 66

SNOUTS 69
Snout Butterfly 70

LONGWINGS 73
Gulf Fritillary 74
Zebra Longwing 76

BRUSHFOOTS 79
Variegated Fritillary 80
Great Spangled Fritillary 82
Pearl Crescent 84
Chalcedon Checkerspot 86
Question Mark 88
Hop Merchant 90

Mourning Cloak 92
Milbert's Tortoise Shell 94
American Painted Lady 96
Painted Lady 98
West Coast Lady 100
Red Admiral 102
Buckeye 104
White Admiral 106
Red-spotted Purple 108
Viceroy 110
Lorquin's Admiral 112
California Sister 114
Goatweed Butterfly 116
Hackberry Butterfly 118

SATYRS, BROWNS AND WOOD NYMPHS   121
Common Wood Nymph 122

MONARCHS AND QUEENS   125
Monarch 126
Queen 128

GLOSSARY   130

INDEX   132

DEDICATION

One man has been the driving force to keep this yellow and black swallowtail from almost sure extinction.

The Schaus' Swallowtail, a large, slow-flying butterfly, once thrived in Miami and throughout the Florida Keys. But urban sprawl wiped out most of its forest home by the early 1900s. Then, in the 1970s, spraying pesticides for mosquitos shrank the number of these swallowtails from about 10,000 to just a few dozen.

One man has been the driving force to prevent spraying pesticides in the Schaus' forest home in Spring, when these butterflies lay their eggs and their caterpillars hatch and feed.

In 1977, the federal government listed the butterfly on the endangered species list. One man, a university research scientist and world-wide authority on butterflies, wanted to capture a few of the butterflies in the wild, let them lay eggs, and rear them in his research lab. His idea was to reintroduce the Schaus' Swallowtail to new south Florida sites.

One man has been the driving force for eight years to petition the government for the permits needed to capture and rear an endangered species.

Years were invested in rearing the butterflies and the thousands of host plants needed by their caterpillars. In Spring 1996, hundreds of Schaus' Swallowtails were released at south Florida sites. They have been mating and laying eggs and, now, the butterfly is making a comeback. It could be the second American species (after the Bald Eagle) ever to be taken off the endangered species list. The U.S. Postal Service has even featured the Schaus' on a postage stamp.

One man has made a difference.

We dedicate this book to Thomas Emmel, Zoologist, University of Florida.

SCHAUS' SWALLOWTAIL   *Heraclides aristodemus ponceanus*

INTRODUCTION
Butterfly Magic

What prompts my passion for butterflies? Why do I watch them, plant gardens for them, raise them — even plan vacations around them?

Several years ago, during a visit to Butterfly World, a butterfly conservatory in Fort Lauderdale, Florida, I found myself standing in one of its lushly landscaped rooms with dozens and dozens of butterflies all around me. One butterfly in particular caught my eye: a lovely brown and yellow one. It appeared to be on a mission, flitting and flying around one particular shrub.

A sign posted nearby read:

PALAMEDES SWALLOWTAILS LAY EGGS ON THIS SHRUB

Suddenly I wanted nothing more than to see a butterfly — hopefully this butterfly — lay an egg. I bobbed and weaved, following the butterfly's progress around the bush. Once, twice, three times she landed on a leaf — only to immediately fly out a short way and return.

The butterfly landed a fourth time. She paused. She curved her abdomen down. It touched the leaf.

Out came an egg — a round, yellow egg. A very, very, tiny, round, yellow egg.

First I was amazed, then came my questions: Will something eat this butterfly egg? Does a caterpillar or a chrysalis hatch out of an egg? How many eggs will the butterfly lay? How many survive?

Dozens of questions popped into my mind. And that was the beginning of my life with butterflies.

I chuckle when I realize how little I understood about butterflies then. Since that time, I've answered many of those questions through research and experience — for myself, for the many men, women and children who now attend my butterfly lectures, for my friends who receive my butterfly "gifts," and for my husband, Milt.

Milt, a professional photographer, has joined me in this passion that now takes up our entire front yard. Our butterfly garden, tended by me and photographed by him, has attracted over 40 different species of butterflies, many of which lay their eggs on our host plants.

Now we would like to share what we've learned with you in hopes that you, too, will decide that butterflies are amazing.

P. P.

SWALLOWTAILS
Papilionidae

Named for   Tailed hind wings that suggest the tail of a swallow
Cold Weather Stage   All North American species overwinter as chrysalises
Species Worldwide   Approximately 600   **In North America**   Approximately 25

Butterfly Description
Size   Medium to large; our largest butterflies
Color   Some of the most colorful
Flight   Slow and gliding when moving from flower to flower; strong and rapid when disturbed
Walking Legs   Six
Proboscis Length   Most long
Feeds At   Flowers, dung, urine
Males Puddle at Damp Ground?   Yes
Mate Location Method   Most males patrol; some perch
Basking Position   Wings spread
Resting Position   Wings held over back

Egg Description   Round; usually laid singly

Caterpillar Description   Has forked gland, called an *osmeterium,* stored just behind the head; when molested, the caterpillar thrusts the gland out, releasing a foul-smelling odor; sometimes this deters the attacker. Young caterpillars of many species look like bird droppings.

Chrysalis Description   Hangs upright, supported by a silken loop around the middle; it resembles a bit of leaf or wood.

Left: Black Swallowtail

PIPE-VINE SWALLOWTAIL   *Battus philenor*
Wingspan Average   3¾"

His metallic blue hind wings shimmering with iridescence, a male Pipe-vine Swallowtail rests. Females have noticeably less blue. The bodies of these coal-black butterflies are tough and bite-resistant. This allows them to survive after being tasted. Few birds and other predators care to eat Pipe-vine Swallowtails since they are poisonous. Several other butterfly species mimic the Pipe-vine's blue and black color combination hoping to fool predators that they, too, are poisonous. These species include the Spicebush, Black Swallowtail, and Red-spotted Purple.

Holding a leaf with its true legs while hugging the leaf's stem with its fleshy false legs, a Pipe-vine Swallowtail caterpillar dines on pipe-vine. Caterpillars use their three pairs of true legs, located near the head, to hold food. They use

their five pairs of false legs, located behind their true legs, for walking and clinging. Even though false legs are used for walking, they are called "false" because developmentally, they do not carry over through the chrysalis stage to the adult butterfly. The true legs do.

SWALLOWTAILS

ZEBRA SWALLOWTAIL   *Eurytides marcellus*
Wingspan Average   3"

Swordlike tails trailing, a Zebra Swallowtail feeds at shallow milkweed blooms. This butterfly can't nectar at long-tubed flowers since its proboscis is surprisingly short for its size. This species has two seasonal forms and this is the summer form. The spring form is paler, smaller, and has shorter tails.

Birds, lizards, and wasps consider chrysalises tasty meals. Since chrysalises have no means of escaping enemies, their main defense is concealment. Swallowtails make chrysalises in two color forms to better hide themselves.

In summer, if a swallowtail caterpillar makes its chrysalis near green leaves, it makes a green chrysalis. But if it is on something brown, such as a tree trunk or fence post, it makes a brown one. Chrysalises made in the fall usually don't produce a butterfly until after winter. Since there is little greenery for camouflage during winter, fall chrysalises are always brown.

Black Swallowtail
Papilio polyxenes

Wingspan Average   3"

While Black Swallowtails are not as large as some other members of their family, they are widely recognized because they often visit herb gardens to lay eggs on parsley, dill, and fennel. Black Swallowtails sometimes live as long as 35 to 40 days, but they average only 10 to 12 days.

Not bothering to hide in a nest or even among leaves, a leaf-green Black Swallowtail caterpillar sits in the open on fennel. It depends on its cryptic coloring to blend it into its parsley family hosts.

Over millions of years, these plants evolved to produce toxins to kill insects that ate them. But Black Swallowtail caterpillars evolved right along with the plants. They successfully developed ways of detoxifying these plant chemicals and eliminating them from their bodies.

ANISE SWALLOWTAIL *Papilio zelicaon*
Wingspan Average 2¾"

"Western Parsley Swallowtail" is another name for this butterfly since, like the Black Swallowtail, it lays eggs on plants of the parsley family. Anise, also known as Sweet Fennel, is a plant in this family. This lemon-yellow and black butterfly is probably the most common swallowtail west of the Rockies.

For years, butterfly scientists (lepidopterists) wondered about the long, hair-like scales near the wings' bases. They theorized that these scales wafted pheromones through the air or, maybe, detected sensations. But they now know that this "hairiness" helps the butterfly absorb and retain heat.

Attached to the site where it will transform into a butterfly, an Anise Swallowtail caterpillar rests for a day. During this time, its chrysalis skin forms under its caterpillar skin.

GIANT SWALLOWTAIL   *Heraclides cresphontes*
Wingspan Average   4½"

A Giant Swallowtail flutters its wings while feeding. One theory holds that swallowtails do this to keep their balance. Another says that they flutter to keep their full weight off the flower to avoid tipping it and causing its nectar to spill.

This butterfly is one of the three largest in North America. The Tiger and Thoas Swallowtails are the two others.

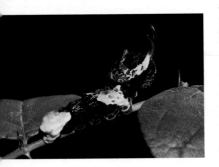

After being disturbed, a Giant Swallowtail caterpillar thrusts out a bright red, forked gland and brushes an irritant on its assailant. In addition, the gland releases a foul smell. Sometimes, this deters its assailant. The caterpillar usually keeps the gland stored in a pocket behind his head. Only swallowtails have such glands, called *osmeteria*.

TIGER SWALLOWTAIL *Pterourus glaucus*

Wingspan Average 4½"

A large, black-striped Tiger Swallowtail carefully works over tightly clustered blooms looking for nectar. This impressive butterfly is one of the most well-known in North America, and it has a counterpart in the western states, the Western Tiger Swallowtail (shown in orange). It prefers to nectar at flowers four feet or more off the ground. However, it will visit shorter flowers, especially if they are as nectar-rich as those of Butterfly Bush (*Buddleia* spp.). The butterfly's striking blue band identifies it as a female since the male lacks the blue band. Males and females of many species look different from each other.

The bark like brown chrysalis of a Tiger Swallowtail comes complete with its own green "lichen" camouflage. A chrysalis is a small, hard case in which a caterpillar transforms into a butterfly.

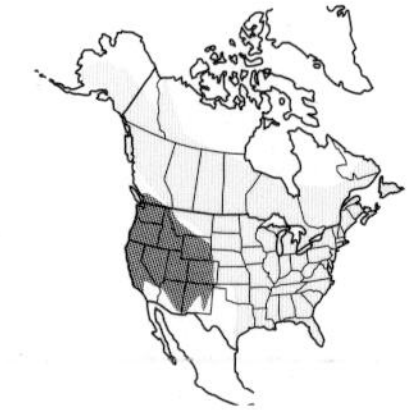

SPICEBUSH SWALLOWTAIL *Pterourus troilus*

Wingspan Average   4"

Looking very different thousands of years ago, these tasty butterflies were constantly under attack. Then, one emerged from its chrysalis looking ever so slightly like the toxic Pipe-vine Swallowtail. At least it looked enough like it to cause a bird to hesitate in its attack — allowing the butterfly to escape.

The butterfly passed on its "helpful" color genes. Most of its offspring looked "normal" and birds attacked them as usual. But some had variations of its coloring. A few mimicked the toxic butterfly better than the others. They, too, fooled their attackers for a while. They outlived their "normal" siblings, giving them more time to pass on their "helpful" genes.

Looking fearsome, a Spicebush Swallowtail caterpillar wears a snake disguise to warn off enemies. The "head" and "eyes" are fakes. The caterpillar holds its head under the fake one.

WHITES AND SULPHURS
Pieridae

Named for   Their dominant color: white, yellow, or orange
Cold Weather Stage   Varies with species; may be adult, chrysalis, or caterpillar
Species Worldwide   Approximately 1,000   **In North America**   Approximately 60

Butterfly Description
   Size   Small to medium; some large
   Color   White, yellow, or orange
   Flight   Steadily fluttering; no gliding
   Walking Legs   Six
   Proboscis Length   Varies with species
   Feeds At   Flowers
   Males Puddle at Damp Ground?   Yes
   Mate Location Method   In North America, males patrol
   Basking Position   Some hold wings over back and tip sideways to sun's rays; some spread wings; some whites hold wings half open
   Resting Position   Usually with wings held over back

Egg Description   Spindle-shaped; laid singly

Caterpillar Description   Long, green, slender

Chrysalis Description   Triangular; cone-headed; hangs upright, supported by a silken loop around the middle

Left: Cloudless Sulphur

CHECKERED WHITE   *Pontia protodice*
Wingspan Average   1½"

The Checkered White seems to be more abundant in the West now than in pre-colonial times. This is probably due to expanded farming, which disturbs the soil and gives "weedy" members of the mustard family more places to take hold. Plants in the mustard family are host for this butterfly's caterpillars.

The Checkered White's coloring is highly variable; it appears in all shades of brown, tan, gray, or olive. This butterfly, which thrives in open, disturbed landscapes like fields, vacant lots, and roadsides, has a lifespan of only seven days.

CABBAGE BUTTERFLY *Pieris rapae*

Wingspan Average 1½"

A Cabbage Butterfly has chosen a roost for the night. The butterflies of most species roost alone.

Watch a Cabbage Butterfly as it approaches flowers to nectar. It often uncoils its proboscis before it even lands!

This common butterfly is not a native of North America. It was unintentionally introduced from Europe about 1860. Within 30 short years it populated most of the United States and Canada. Perhaps interstate shipments of cabbages helped foster the rapid spread of this butterfly since cabbages are one of the butterfly's host plants. Many butterflies do not adapt well to human settings but this butterfly is an exception.

SARA ORANGE TIP *Anthocharis sara*
Wingspan Average 1½"

With wings half open, a Sara Orange Tip stands on two Forget-Me-Not flowers to gain access to nectar.

Most often, patterns on upper and under wings look different from each other because they have different purposes. Butterflies use upper wing patterns to aid in mate selection. These patterns, visible during flight, help the butterfly distinguish between species and sexes. While a butterfly rests, however, it holds its wings over its back and only its under wing shows. This under wing pattern helps blend the butterfly into its surroundings and hide it from danger.

This butterfly frequents pastures, hay fields, mountain roads, and many other sunny places. An early spring butterfly, the Sara Orange Tip flies low to the ground. Some compare its flight to seeing two orange flags fluttering in the breeze. The female, lacking the orange tips, is all white or all yellow above.

ALFALFA BUTTERFLY   *Colias eurytheme*
Wingspan Average   2"

Alfalfa Butterfly females appear in two color forms: bright yellow and white. White butterflies of this species are always females. They develop faster than their yellow sisters. And since they also have more fat and larger eggs, they have a reproductive advantage.

A yellow female results when a caterpillar uses all its nitrogen stores to make yellow pigment for wings. A white female results when a caterpillar uses some of its nitrogen to speed up its growth. The butterfly's genes determine how it will use the nitrogen.

An Alfalfa Butterfly is often superabundant in alfalfa fields and clover meadows. It lays eggs on both plants and the caterpillars are occasional pests of these crops. Yellow form females have one reproductive advantage over their white sisters: males, which are always yellow, seem to prefer to mate with yellow females. White and Yellow form females also occur in Cloudless Sulphurs.

DOG FACE   *Zerene cesonia*
Wingspan Average   2¼"

A male Dog Face carries a female during mating. Butterfly matings usually last 30 to 40 minutes, but, in some species, can last up to three hours. When a mated pair is startled, one of the butterflies flies off — carrying the other dangling beneath it. The dangling butterfly often remains passive.

A Dog Face chrysalis is about to produce a butterfly. Some chrysalises, like this one, become transparent a few hours before a butterfly emerges. The poodle-head profile that gives this species its name shows clearly on the butterfly's upper wing. But once the butterfly emerges and dries its wings, it will hold its wings over its back and the poodle design won't be visible.

CLOUDLESS SULPHUR *Phoebis sennae*

Wingspan Average 2½"

"Butter flies" may owe their common name to a butter-yellow species like this one. The Cloudless Sulphur is one of the easiest butterflies to identify. Studies show that this butterfly's eyesight is sensitive to the longest red wavelengths. This may make them prefer red flowers. Butterflies such as the Buckeye, Mourning Cloak, and Hackberry are not able to see these wavelengths.

Wearing a safety belt of tough silk thread around its middle, this Cloudless Sulphur's chrysalis aims head downward. Although the cone shape suggests that the butterfly will emerge with a pointed head, it will not. The butterfly's wings are developing in the enormous rounded section known as a wing case.

BARRED YELLOW   *Eurema daira*
Wingspan Average   1¼"

Two seasonal forms, summer (left) and winter (right) of the Barred Yellow mate. Interestingly, because these butterflies emerged from their chrysalises in different seasons, their life expectancies vary dramatically. The summer white butterfly, a male, will probably live only two days, but may survive up to nine. The winter yellow female may live as long as four or five months. It passes the cool, winter months in its subtropical home, resting and nectaring. It waits to mate until Spring.

A small Barred Yellow approaches an egg-laden Joint Vetch plant (*Aeschynomene*) to lay another egg. Female butterflies search out certain plants on which to lay eggs. These plants that host caterpillars differ for each butterfly species. The hosts contain the exact chemicals that the caterpillars of that species need to thrive. In the wild, Barred Yellows lay only one to a few eggs per plant before moving on. This female has laid so many eggs on this one plant because she is in captivity and it is the only plant available to her.

SLEEPY ORANGE   *Eurema nicippe*
Wingspan Average   1½"

A Sleepy Orange nectars. Contrary to its name, it does not act sleepy when it's on the move. It has a rapid and zigzag flight. Every summer, some Sleepy Oranges migrate north from their southern home. Cold winters later kill these emigrants. In the South, though, offspring of the remaining butterflies spend the winter resting quietly and, sometimes, feeding. Perhaps that's how the butterfly came by its name.

A fuzzy Sleepy Orange caterpillar explores its food plant, *Cassia.* The Sleepy Orange doesn't depend on armor to protect it from predators. Nor does it hide in a tent. Rather, the caterpillar's color matches its food plant so well that the caterpillar is easily overlooked.

GOSSAMER WINGS
Lycaenidae

Named for   Dainty, delicate wings
Cold Weather Stage   Varies with species; may be chrysalis, caterpillar or egg
Species Worldwide   Approximately 7,000   **In North America**   Approximately 100

Butterfly Description
Size   Small
Color   Most colorful; iridescent blues and fiery reds and oranges are common; some are gray or brown
Flight   Rapid
Walking Legs   Males, four; females, six
Proboscis Length   Most short
Feeds At   Flowers
Males Puddle at Damp Ground?   Some, yes
Mate Location Method   Most males perch; some patrol
Basking Position   Wings spread
Resting Position   Wings held over back

Egg Description   Turban-shaped; usually laid singly

Caterpillar Description   Oval-shaped with flattened underside; some species have honeydew glands; ants collect honeydew made by caterpillar; in turn, ants protect caterpillars by swarming over caterpillar predators

Chrysalis Description   Many can make faint noises; scientists believe these sounds may help ward off predatory ants; usually formed in ground litter; silken thread may attach it to a support

Left: Little Copper

LITTLE COPPER *Lycaena phlaeas*
Wingspan Average 1"

In the East, the Little Copper populates many areas disturbed by man: vacant lots, yards, old fields, and roadsides. The butterfly frequents these places because its caterpillar's primary food plant, a weed called sheep sorrel, thrives in these areas.

"Flame Copper" is one of this little butterfly's names. Typical of many butterflies, Little Coppers live only about 14 days. There's no time to waste in reproducing. Females, which look similar to males, often mate within a day of emerging from the chrysalis. Males must usually mature for a day or so.

PURPLISH COPPER *Epidemia helloides*
Wingspan Average   1"

A Purplish Copper basks in early morning sunlight. Since the butterfly spent the night with wings held over its back, dew collected on their undersides. Now it spreads its wings to both dry them and warm himself. This butterfly may appear frail but it endures late into autumn. Coppers are a group of butterflies with iridescent orange or red wings with some dark markings.

This is the most widespread copper in North America. It even occurs in many areas of the Northwest which lack many butterfly species. The Purplish Copper frequents a variety of habitats, many of them moist — damp meadows, tidal marshes, stream sides, and weedy city fields. This butterfly feeds only at flowers.

GRAY HAIRSTREAK *Strymon melinus*

Wingspan Average   1"

Hairlike tails resembling antennas and hind wing spots resembling eyes are hairstreak characteristics. To more fully complete its false head impersonation, the hairstreak often rubs its wings together while perching or nectaring. This causes the tails to move like real antennas. The purpose of the hairstreak's false head is to draw a predator's attention away from the vulnerable real head. In an attack, the butterfly loses a piece of its hind wing, but it will probably survive to fly another day.

While most butterflies lay eggs on only a handful of plants, the Gray Hairstreak lays on an incredibly wide variety — almost 50 different plants in 20 different families. Owing to this adaptability, the Gray Hairstreak is the most widespread hairstreak in North America. It thrives in open, sunny places such as gardens, parks, open fields, and even vacant lots.

EASTERN TAILED BLUE   *Everes comyntas*
Wingspan Average   ¾"

Balanced atop plant spines, an Eastern Tailed Blue soaks up heat from the sun's rays. While many species bask by spreading their wings, this little butterfly basks by holding its wings at about a 45 degree angle.

The Eastern Tailed Blue, one of our smallest butterflies, could hide behind a dime. It might seem that such a small butterfly would be hard to find but, due to its abundance, it is not. It is one of the East's most common butterflies. Look for it around clover, its host plant, at roadsides and rights-of-way. Its counterpart in the west is the Western Tailed Blue (shown in orange).

Salts concentrate on ground where water regularly accumulates and then evaporates. Male butterflies of some species need these salts. They also need to replace fluids lost, perhaps, while searching for a mate. When one male locates sodium on damp ground, others gather. This gathering is called a puddle club.

SPRING AZURE   *Celastrina argiolus*
Wingspan Average 1"

A Spring Azure feeds at one of its favorite nectar sources, small white flowers. The Spring Azure is one of our tiniest butterflies and one of our shortest-lived. Females mate on their first day out of the chrysalis, lay eggs on the second, and may not even live to see the third. This is one of the first butterflies to emerge in the spring.

Signaling that she does not want to mate, a female Spring Azure lifts her abdomen so that a male cannot join with her. When females do not want to mate, it usually means they have mated already. However, courting males do not give up pursuit easily. Most courtships do not result in butterflies mating.

SNOUTS
Libytheidae

Named for   Long mouth parts that project forward
Cold Weather Stage   Disputed
Species Worldwide   Less than a dozen   **In North America**   1

Butterfly Description
  Size   Medium
  Color   Brown or orange-brown; some are blue
  Flight   Fairly strong
  Walking Legs   Males, four; females, six
  Proboscis Length   Fairly short
  Feeds At   Small flowers, bird droppings
  Males Puddle at Damp Ground?   Yes
  Mate Location Method   Disputed
  Basking Position   Wings spread
  Resting Position   Wings held over back

Egg Description   Oval, ridged

Caterpillar Description   Green, cylinder-shaped; no spines or horns; grows quickly

Chrysalis Description   Angular; hangs upside down by tail hooks

Left: Snout Butterfly

SNOUT BUTTERFLY   *Libytheana bachmanii*
Wingspan Average   1¾"

This butterfly has been misnamed since it does not actually have a snout. Instead, the Snout Butterfly has a pair of tremendously long palpi, hairy projections in front of the eyes. Palpi are sensory organs, detecting odors for mating (pheromones) and feeding. Perhaps at one time the Snout Butterfly's unusually developed palpi served an additional useful purpose but they have no obvious special function today. Most butterflies carry their palpi both in front of *and below* the eyes and they are hardly noticeable.

With its "neck" arched, the Snout Butterfly caterpillar at left prepares to shed first its rigid head capsule and then its skin. The head capsules cannot grow in size so, like the skin, caterpillars must shed them periodically. The sibling at right has just shed its head capsule and skin and even wears a new color pattern to prove it. Caterpillars' colors and markings often look remarkably different from stage to stage.

LONGWINGS
Heliconiidae

Named for   Long, narrow forewings that are twice as long as wide
Cold Weather Stage   Cannot survive cold in any life stage; adults in south overwinter; in summer, offspring progressively migrate north
Species Worldwide   Approximately 75   **In North America**   Seven

Butterfly Description
Size   Medium
Color   Bright colors advertise their distastefulness
Flight   Most flutter slowly
Walking Legs   Four
Proboscis Length   Average
Feeds At   Flowers; some species feed on pollen
Males Puddle at Damp Ground?   Not usually
Mate Location Method   Males patrol
Basking Position   Wings spread
Resting Position   Wings held over back

Egg Description   Long, rounded; most laid singly; some in clusters

Caterpillar Description   Many branching spines on body and head

Chrysalis Description   Angular; hangs upside down by tail hooks

Left: Gulf Fritillary

GULF FRITILLARY   *Agraulis vanillae*
Wingspan Average   2¾"

A Gulf Fritillary probes for nectar with his proboscis. Many flower nectar tubes, like those of this Mexican Sunflower, have minute openings. The butterfly needs unusually fine control of its proboscis to search out these openings. Microscopic muscles inside the proboscis provide that control. This butterfly makes its home all around the Gulf of Mexico and throughout the south, hence its name.

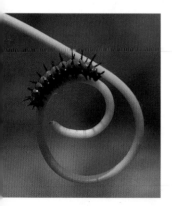

The sausage-like appearance of this caterpillar indicates it is outgrowing its skin. Stretch detectors in its joints will soon signal its brain that it is time to grow a new roomier skin under this one. After the caterpillar grows the new skin, enzymes will partially dissolve this old one. The caterpillar will wriggle out of the remains.

ZEBRA LONGWING   *Heliconius charitonius*
Wingspan Average   3"

A Zebra at rest, left.

Nectaring at flowers, a Zebra's proboscis collects pollen. Later, the Zebra perches, his pollen-decorated proboscis coiled. He releases a drop of saliva onto the pollen, dissolving it to a liquid. Then he drinks up the liquid. By feeding on protein-rich pollen, the Zebra lives up to three months, about six times as long as the average butterfly. Only Zebras and their Heliconian cousins can feed on pollen.

A Zebra caterpillar winds his way along a passion vine. Zebras eat the toxic vines. Unlike Black Swallowtails that eliminate the poisons they eat, Zebras store poisons in their bodies. The poisonous caterpillars then sicken vertebrates like birds and lizards that prey on them. The vertebrates won't eat black and white caterpillars after getting sick on one or two. The poison does not affect invertebrates like assassin bugs and wasps, however.

BRUSHFOOTS
Nymphalidae

Named for   Tiny forelegs
Cold Weather Stage   Varies with species; may be adult, caterpillar or chrysalis
Species Worldwide   Approximately 4,500   **In North America**   Approximately 185

Butterfly Description
   Size   Small to large; most here are medium
   Color   Orange, yellow, black, and brown are common; striking patterns
   Flight   Most have rapid flight
   Walking Legs   Four
   Proboscis Length   Fairly short
   Feeds At   Flowers, sap, dung, rotting fruit, animal carcasses
   Males Puddle at Damp Ground?   Not usually
   Mate Location Method   Males of some species perch; others patrol
   Basking Position   Most bask with wings spread
   Resting Position   Wings held over back

Egg Description   Barrel-shaped; laid singly or in clusters

Caterpillar Description   Many are spiny; some feed in groups when young

Chrysalis Description   Most hang upside down by tail hooks

Left: Red-spotted Purple

Variegated Fritillary

Euptoieta claudia

Wingspan Average   2"

Because the Variegated Fritillary's caterpillar feeds on both violets and passion vines, the species has characteristics of both fritillaries and longwings. Fritillaries feed almost exclusively on violets, however; and longwings feed on poisonous passion vines. So this butterfly is neither a true fritillary nor a longwing. This species proves that, when working with nature, we can't often draw hard and fast artificial lines.

Its skin stretched maximally, a caterpillar will soon shed its skin for the last time. A caterpillar's skin is inelastic so, as it grows, it must periodically shed its old skin for a new one. Because a caterpillar produces juvenile hormone during its early and middle stages, a caterpillar molts into another caterpillar. But when the caterpillar is large enough, juvenile-hormone production stops. When it molts this time, the caterpillar will molt into a chrysalis.

GREAT SPANGLED FRITILLARY   *Speyeria cybele*
Wingspan Average   2½"

A Great Spangled Fritillary nectars at one of its favorite flowers, thistles. Many factors determine which flowers are a butterfly's favorites. The prime factor is proboscis length. Butterflies with a short proboscis simply can't reach nectar in long flower tubes. Another factor is flower height. Larger butterflies, such as this one, prefer taller flowers. And a few species prefer certain flower colors over others.

Closeup view of this Great Spangled Fritillary's underwing, top.

Overlapping like roof shingles, millions of scales cover a Great Spangled Fritillary's underwing. Each scale's center is hollow, perhaps to reduce weight. Scales are so tiny that about 500 can fit side-by-side on a one-inch line. When a butterfly is handled, scales, which resemble a fine, colored powder, come off easily. The most often asked question about butterflies may be whether a butterfly can still fly when it loses scales. It can.

PEARL CRESCENT   *Phyciodes tharos*

Wingspan Average   1¼"

A male Pearl Crescent waits for a female to happen by. Like butterflies of all species that use this lay-in-wait method of finding females, males dart out at anything that flutters by — wasps, dragonflies, even birds. Some say this means that these males are combative or even territorial. It more likely means that these butterflies need to approach fluttering objects to investigate whether they are females of the appropriate species. In detecting movement, butterflies' eyes are better than a human's; in judging shape and pattern, they are much poorer.

A female Pearl Crescent warms her flight muscles by basking. The colorful Pearl Crescent is a common and familiar butterfly. The first generation appears in April; successive generations fly all summer long and into fall. This low-flying butterfly frequents meadows, open fields, roadsides, and gardens.

CHALCEDON CHECKERSPOT   *Euphydryas chalcedona*

Wingspan Average   1¾"

Male and female Chalcedon Checkerspots mate. During mating, the male (left) passes sperm to the female. In this species, females do not have to wait a day or so after mating to start laying eggs. They can begin immediately. The female is noticeably larger than her mate and this is typical of many species. Females are larger because they carry a heavy cargo of several hundred eggs. Since they weigh more than males, they fly more slowly.

Seeming to defy the law of gravity, a black, spiny Chalcedon Checkerspot clings upside down to a leaf. Caterpillars can hang upside down and walk up and down vertical stems because each of their ten fleshy false legs is tipped with dozens of tiny "fishhooks" called crochets. With each step, crochets hook into the leaf. The caterpillar can even sleep upside down without fear of falling off the plant.

QUESTION MARK *Polygonia interrogationis*
Wingspan Average 2½"

Different species of butterflies pass the winter in various life stages. For instance, swallowtails pass the winter in the chrysalis. The Question Mark and its close relative, the Hop Merchant, pass the winter as adult butterflies. While some of their kind migrate south, some stay behind to face the cold. They seek shelter in tree crevices, hollow logs, and stone piles where they remain quiet for days, even weeks, at a time. On warm winter days, they may come out and fly around.

Aptly named for the unique silvery "question mark" on its hindwing, a Question Mark feeds on dung. While not usually thought of as a food source, dung provides protein that nectar often lacks. The dung of meat-eating animals, such as fox or coyote, is especially appealing to some male butterflies.

A chain of Question Mark eggs dangles from a leaf. Question Mark eggs are often laid in chains of three to ten eggs. There is a defensive reason for stacking eggs in columns. Predators prey less on those eggs in the middle.

HOP MERCHANT
Polygonia comma
Wingspan Average   2"

One of nature's little recyclers, a Hop Merchant sips the juice of a fallen apple. Many butterflies in the Brushfoot family specialize in feeding on fallen fruit, tree sap, carrion, and dung. Unlike nectar, these foods do not require a long proboscis to access them — so these butterflies never evolved the longer proboscis of many nectar-feeding butterflies. Considering the size of the butterflies in this family, their proboscises are quite short.

The Hop Merchant and Question Mark are anglewing butterflies, named for their wings' ragged edges. The upper wings of Anglewings are always red-orange. Their underwings always have a bark-like resemblance. When disturbed, Anglewings perch head down on tree trunks and close their wings, blending into the background perfectly.

MOURNING CLOAK   *Nymphalis antiopa*
Wingspan Average   3¼"

Many people recognize this conspicuous butterfly but may not know its name. With a life span of 10 months, the Mourning Cloak is likely the longest-lived butterfly in North America. Like the Question Mark and Hop Merchant, it seeks out hollow trees and loose bark in which to hibernate during winter. Surprisingly, it also hibernates during summer. When adults emerge from the chrysalis in June or July, they feed for only a few days before seeking shelter and resting until fall. Then they come out and feed, storing energy for their winter hibernation.

Preparing to make a chrysalis, a Mourning Cloak caterpillar hangs in a "J" and rests while its chrysalis skin forms under its caterpillar skin. Its caterpillar skin split, it wriggles to shed the skin. It discards its 10 orange false legs, too, since they will be of no use to it as a butterfly.

Because a new chrysalis is soft, it is especially open to attack by parasites — wasps and flies that try to lay their eggs in it. But the chrysalis soon hardens, making it more difficult to penetrate.

MILBERT'S TORTOISE SHELL *Aglais milberti*

Wingspan Average 1¾"

The flame-like bands of this small butterfly make it unmistakable. It looks different, though, after if hibernates all winter in hollow trees and abandoned buildings. When it appears in March, it is usually pale and tattered. Milbert's Tortoise Shell underwing is a perfect example of protective coloration. Resting on a tree trunk with wings held over its back, the butterfly is very hard to detect.

A Milber'ts Tortoise Shell lays up to 700 eggs at a time on the underside of nettles. Very few butterfly species lay eggs in tremendously huge clusters like this. The defensive strategy in laying so many eggs is that while predators may eat many, some will survive. Only an average of two offspring from a mating pair of butterflies live to reproduce — regardless of the species.

AMERICAN PAINTED LADY
Vanessa virginiensis

Wingspan Average   2"

Two large blue eyespots and a vivid pink forewing patch distinguish the American Painted Lady from its cousins — the Painted Lady and West Coast Lady. They have upper wings that look similar to this butterfly's but they have only small eyespots below. It is unclear whether this butterfly can survive cold winters. Migrants from the south may have to recolonize the north each year. The Mourning Cloak, Milbert's Tortoise Shell and some other butterflies do survive freezing winters.

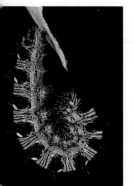

An American Painted Lady caterpillar hangs in a "J," preparing to change into a chrysalis. Typical of species in the Brushfoot family, the American Painted Lady makes a chrysalis that hangs freely, like a pendant. The Anise Swallowtail caterpillar is at the same stage of its development. Since it is a Swallowtail, it makes a chrysalis that hangs upright, supported by a silken loop around the middle.

PAINTED LADY   *Vanessa cardui*
Wingspan Average   2¼"

Take a good look at this orange butterfly with the black-and-white wing tips, for it is generally acknowledged to be the most widespread butterfly in the world. It is at home in Africa, Europe, Asia, and North America. Its success in populating the globe can be traced directly to the success of its host plant — thistle. This adaptable, spiny-leaved plant produces feathery seeds in great numbers. The slightest wind scatters them and they take hold wherever they find moist soil. Thistle grows over a great part of the world, leading to the success of the Painted Lady.

Its tiny, fiery-orange wings showing clearly through the chrysalis, a Painted Lady butterfly will emerge within hours — perhaps even minutes. To exit the chrysalis, the butterfly inside swallows air. This makes the butterfly bigger and causes the chrysalis to stretch to its splitting point. The chrysalis splits along weakened lines, called cleavage lines, and the butterfly crawls out. The cleavage lines run the length of the antennas, visible here just in front of the wing.

WEST COAST LADY *Vanessa annabella*
Wingspan Average 2"

At first glance, the salmon-orange West Coast Lady looks very much like the Painted Lady. But look closely at the upper wing, half way between the butterfly's head and wing tip. The bar in the black area is orange in this butterfly, but white in the Painted Lady. These two ladies and a third, the American Painted Lady, along with the Red Admiral, are all closely related. They all belong to the same butterfly group (genus), *Vanessa*, so *Vanessa* becomes part of each one's scientific name.

Most flower-visiting butterflies such as the West Coast Lady are not at all finicky about at which flowers to feed. They will visit dozens, even hundreds, of kinds of flowers to find enough nectar. Different flowers produce nectar of different sugar concentrations. Butterflies prefer a thinner nectar than bees, perhaps to avoid clogging the proboscis. Butterflies use nectar to meet their energy needs. No nectar is channeled into butterfly growth because, of course, butterflies do not grow.

RED ADMIRAL   *Vanessa atalanta*
Wingspan Average   2"

A Red Admiral puddles. Why certain male butterflies puddle is not clear. Some scientists say that taking in salt activates the butterfly's temperature-regulating system. The Red Admiral doesn't rely on the basking technique alone to warm itself. It can vibrate its wings slightly for a minute or so to warm the flight muscles. Butterflies using this technique appear to be shivering. Some other butterflies that use this method to warm themselves include Question Mark, Painted Lady, and Monarch.

A leaf nest made of the formidable stinging nettle protects a Red Admiral caterpillar from both the weather and many enemies, including lizards and birds. Because the outer layer of the caterpillar's skin is hardened, the caterpillar itself is not affected by the nettles' irritating hairs. The plant's chemicals have no effect on the hardened skin, nor can the stinging nettles pierce it.

BUCKEYE   *Junonia coenia*
Wingspan Average   2¼"

"The best defense is a good offense" is the motto this butterfly follows. When the Buckeye sits on the ground, its wings held over its back, it resembles a leaf. But when molested by a bird, it flashes open its wings and displays its large, pupiled eyespots. Studies show that the eyespots startle birds who may mistake them for two or more rodents. Male Buckeyes awaiting females often perch on bare ground for hours.

A Buckeye caterpillar, wearing its new skin, has just shrugged out of its old one and left it behind. First, the caterpillar made and laid down enough silk on the leaf to make a pad. Then it grabbed the silk pad with its hindmost pair of legs. While it rested for a day, its new skin formed under the old one. It then pulled its head out of the old head capsule. With its old skin still firmly attached to the silk pad, the caterpillar wriggled forward, leaving his old skin behind. Within minutes, its new spines popped up like periscopes.

WHITE ADMIRAL *Basilarchia arthemis*
Wingspan Average 3"

A male White Admiral "puddles" at sand to obtain needed salts and nutrients. Since the only way a butterfly can obtain nourishment is through its proboscis, extracting minerals from bare sand may seem impossible. The butterfly solves the dilemma by first spitting out a saliva droplet onto the sand. When the saliva has dissolved the minerals, the butterfly simply sips the droplet back up.

Scientists once thought that the White Admiral and the Red-spotted Purple were two separate species. Genetic evidence has shown, however, that they are two geographic forms of the same species. Northern ranges are home to the White Admiral form and southern ranges are home to the Red-spotted Purple. In the south, this butterfly's range overlaps the range of the poisonous Pipe-vine Swallowtail. Scientists believe southern butterflies of this species gained protection by gradually evolving to impersonate the poisonous butterfly.

RED-SPOTTED PURPLE   *Basilarchia arthemis astyanax*
Wingspan Average   3¼"

A male Red-spotted Purple perches and waits for a female to pass by. All species use one of two behaviors, rarely both, to locate mates — perching and patrolling. Males that perch go to certain places (such as hilltops) at certain times of the day (such as mornings), perch, and await females. Males that patrol, like Tiger Swallowtails and Monarchs, fly almost constantly, searching out females.

A Red-spotted Purple preparing to lay an egg flutters around branches of her host plant, typically wild cherry. She selects a leaf at the top of a branch that is 12 feet to 30 feet high. Then she lands just above the selected leaf. While backing up, she probes with her abdomen and lays a round, gray, dimpled egg, usually at the very tip of the leaf. Since spiders, ants and flies constantly search leaf surfaces for eggs and tiny insects, a butterfly egg is less likely to be discovered at the leaf's tip or edge than on the broad surface.

VICEROY   *Basilarchia archippus*
Wingspan Average   2¾"

Viceroys look so similar to Monarchs that many find it difficult to tell them apart. (Viceroys have a black line across their hindwings.) For years we thought Viceroys were tasty butterflies whose resemblance to the poisonous Monarch tricked birds into thinking that they, too, were poisonous. We now know that Viceroys themselves are distasteful and birds would have avoided them anyway. Viceroys could have evolved their own unique color pattern advertising their distastefulness, but they mimicked the Monarch's. What advantage could this have for the Viceroy? Simple — birds must learn to avoid only one pattern, not two.

Monarchs do not summer in Florida and the southwest. So in those places, instead of mimicking orange Monarchs that aren't present, Viceroys mimic chestnut-brown Queens that are. Queens, close relatives of Monarchs, are also poisonous.

LORQUIN'S ADMIRAL   *Basilarchia lorquini*
Wingspan Average   2½"

The rust-orange wing tips of the Lorquin's Admiral serve the same purpose as the hindwings of the Gray Hairstreak. They divert a predator's attention away from the vital head and body. In addition, the butterfly's bold cream-colored stripes actually help to break up the recognizable butterfly outline, making the butterfly more difficult for predators to spot. Several butterflies, including the Zebra, Tiger, Giant and Schaus' Swallowtails, use this defensive pattern, known as disruptive coloration.

Clinging to its chrysalis, a newly emerged Lorquin's Admiral hangs its wings, allowing them to expand and dry. When butterflies emerge from the chrysalis, they are perfectly formed — except for their tiny, crumpled wings. Chrysalises would have to be enormous to fit full-size wings. Even when fully expanded, a new butterfly's wings are floppy. The butterfly waits an hour or more for them to harden before taking its first flight.

CALIFORNIA SISTER   *Adelpha bredowii*

Wingspan Average   3"

A male California Sister puddles at a creek bank, drawing sodium and amino acids from the mud. These two elements are essential if sperm are to mature. In studies where female butterflies could mate only with males that had not puddled, the females produced far fewer fertile eggs than they normally do.

A mature California Sister caterpillar will soon make its chrysalis. It is a myth that a butterfly develops entirely within the chrysalis. From the time it hatches from an egg, a caterpillar is slowly changing into a butterfly. The changes are not noticed, though, because they happen inside the caterpillar. For example, inside this caterpillar, the adult's antennas and proboscis are growing rapidly. By the time it makes its chrysalis, the major changes to the adult form will already be made.

GOATWEED BUTTERFLY   *Anaea andria*

Wingspan Average   2¾"

This fiery orange-red butterfly takes its name from its host plant, goatweed (*Croton*). Its wing color underneath is a mottled brown. When it lands on the underside of a twig and holds its wings over its back, the Goatweed Butterfly easily passes for a dead leaf. A bird chasing this butterfly follows its orange flashing wings. But when the butterfly abruptly lands and mimics a leaf, it seems to suddenly disappear. The bird retains the original search for an orange butterfly and can't rapidly adjust to the new dead leaf.

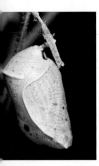

A thick, light green Goatweed Butterfly chrysalis vaguely resembles the chrysalises of the Monarch and Queen butterflies. Even as the caterpillar sheds its skin for the last time, the butterfly's wings, proboscis, antennas, and legs pop to the surface of the chrysalis, their shapes plainly visible. Muscles reorganize for flight and cells rearrange themselves. New organs develop. Sperm and many eggs mature. Now, except for having miniature wings, the butterfly is fully developed. A scant ten days has passed since the caterpillar changed into a chrysalis.

HACKBERRY BUTTERFLY *Asterocampa celtis*
Wingspan Average   2"

The bulbous shape of this butterfly's abdomen proclaims that she is a female. The abdomens of females are usually rounder than those of males because females carry a few hundred eggs. Female butterflies emerge from the chrysalis with many fully developed eggs, and some females can produce still more. Lining the left and right sides of the abdomen are tiny holes (not visible here) through which the butterfly takes in and expels air. Butterflies have no lungs, nor do they breathe through the proboscis.

Three Hackberry Butterfly caterpillars dine on leaves of their host, Hackberry trees. Some caterpillars feed singly, but Hackberry Butterfly caterpillars feed in tight groups. They descend on and eat in unison the leaves of one branch. When disturbed, they will even twitch in unison. The sight of many twitching bodies may discourage some predators.

SATYRS, BROWNS & WOOD NYMPHS
Satyridae

Named for   Their mythical namesakes that live in forests and meadows
Cold Weather Stage   Varies with species; may be adult and/or caterpillar
Species Worldwide   Approximately 3,000   **In North America**   Approximately 50

Butterfly Description
  Size   Medium
  Color   Soft browns, grays, rusts
  Flight   Weak, low, erratic
  Walking Legs   Four
  Proboscis Length   Short
  Feeds At   Sap, dung, rotting fruit; sometimes flowers
  Males Puddle at Damp Ground?   Not usually
  Mate Location Method   Most species patrol
  Basking Position   Wings spread
  Resting Position   Wings held over back

Egg Description   Drum-shaped

Caterpillar Description   Slender; forked tail

Chrysalis Description   Hangs upside down by tail hooks from grass stems, leaf litter

Left: Common Wood Nymph

COMMON WOOD NYMPH   *Cercyonis pegala*
Wingspan Average   2½"

A Common Wood Nymph rests on a sunlit leaf. These butterflies often rest in the open, wings held over their backs. When disturbed, they take off but they are not strong flyers. Instead, they fly weakly and erratically until they suddenly light on the underside of a leaf or branch.   With their yellow forewing patch hidden, their brown underwing is excellent at camouflaging them; they are almost impossible to find. Like the Gray Hairstreak's false eyespots, the purpose of Common Wood Nymph's eyespots is to divert attention away from the vital head and body.

A plump, pale green Common Wood Nymph chrysalis hangs from a grass stem. A butterfly's time in the chrysalis usually ranges from one to two weeks. There are exceptions. For instance, most chrysalises made in fall do not produce butterflies until spring, when host plants have leafed out and nectar plants have bloomed.

MONARCHS AND QUEENS
Danaidae

Named for   Royalty
Cold Weather Stage   Adult butterfly
Species Worldwide   Approximately 300   **In North America**   4

Butterfly Description
  Size   Medium to large
  Color   Our species are orange or brown
  Flight   Strong; often glides
  Walking Legs   Four
  Proboscis Length   Average
  Feeds At   Flowers
  Males Puddle at Damp Ground?   No
  Mate Location Method   In North America, males patrol
  Basking Position   Wings spread
  Resting Position   Wings held over back

Egg Description   Cone-shaped; usually laid singly

Caterpillar Description   Brightly striped; fleshy filaments near head and rear

Chrysalis Description   Cylinder-shaped; stout; hangs upside down by tail hooks

Left: Monarch

MONARCH   *Danaus plexippus*
Wingspan Average   3¾"

Even as it nectars, a Monarch advertises to predators that it is distasteful. A butterfly wearing striking color combinations, such as black and orange, is often signaling that it is distasteful and, perhaps, poisonous. Predators learn this by getting sick from one or two brightly colored butterflies, and then avoiding those butterflies with bright colors. Color combinations that warn of bad taste often include black and yellow (Zebra), black and white (Zebra caterpillar), and black and blue (Pipe-vine Swallowtail).

A brightly striped Monarch caterpillar munches a milkweed leaf, absorbing the milkweed's poisons into its own body. The poisons, which remain with the caterpillar through the chrysalis stage and into the adult stage, are its main defense as an adult. Yet, some of the 100 or more milkweeds in North America have only small amounts of poisons. Butterflies that feed on these milkweeds are tasty to predators. Predators cannot tell which Monarchs are tasty so they leave them all alone.

QUEEN   *Danaus gilippus*
Wingspan Average   3¼"

A chestnut-brown Queen nectars at lantana. It's easy to see that the Queen's color pattern and general form are similar to that of its cousin, the Monarch. And like the Monarch caterpillar, the Queen caterpillar feeds on toxic milkweed so the Queen, too, is poisonous. Predators must learn that certain butterflies are poisonous. When they do, they do not automatically learn that the caterpillar and chrysalis life stages are also poisonous. They must learn those lessons separately. Queens are large butterflies and strong fliers.

A plump Queen chrysalis hangs among rosy pink liatris buds. The glossy, jade green chrysalis bears metallic golden dots and a gold-edged band. It looks very similar to a Monarch chrysalis. Butterfly enthusiasts have referred to both as "glass houses with golden nails." Some chrysalises evolved gold adornments so that the chrysalis would look like something other than the juicy tidbit of food it is. "Chrysalis" derives from the Greek word for gold, referring to the fact that some chrysalises are decorated with it.

MONARCHS AND QUEENS

GLOSSARY

Unless otherwise noted, these definitions refer strictly to butterflies.

Basking This is a temperature-regulating technique butterflies use on cool days to raise their body temperature so that they may fly. The most common way butterflies bask is by spreading their wings, and letting the sun shine on their upper wings.

Chrysalis This a small hard case in which a butterfly caterpillar develops into a butterfly. A chrysalis has no means of escaping enemies, so its main defense is concealment. Note: A chrysalis has a skin, not a silk web like a cocoon.

Cocoon This is a silk web enclosing and protecting a moth caterpillar as it develops into a moth. Butterflies do not make cocoons. Skippers are the exception.

Food Plant (See Host)

Genus This is a group of butterfly species. All the butterflies in a genus are more closely related to each other than to any other species. Monarchs (*Danaus plexippus*) and Queens (*Danaus gilippus*)

belong to the genus, *Danaus*. In a butterfly's scientific name, the genus name is easily recognized because it is always capitalized.

Hibernation This is when a butterfly passes winter in a dormant stage. A butterfly in hibernation often seeks shelter under loose bark, in wood piles, or in outbuildings. On warm days it may emerge and fly around. Passing summer in a dormant stage is known as *aestivation*.

Host / Host Plant This is any plant caterpillars eat and on which butterflies normally lay eggs. Hosts are often species specific. For example, the host for the Zebra Swallowtail is paw paw. No other butterfly species lays eggs on paw paw.

Life Cycle This is the series of four stages in the life of a butterfly: egg, caterpillar, chrysalis, and adult. The length of the life cycle, from egg to adult, varies with each species. It may be as little as a few weeks or as much as two to three years.

Migration   This refers to adult butterflies flying many miles from where they hatched from the egg. They migrate to breed and feed.

Molt   This is the process by which a caterpillar sheds its outgrown skin to reveal a new, more elastic skin underneath. A caterpillar typically molts four to five times.

Nectar   This is the sugary liquid that some flowers produce to attract pollinators.

Patrolling   This is a mate-locating behavior used by some species where males fly almost constantly to search out females. Monarchs and Cloudless Sulphurs are patrolling species.

Perching   This is a mate-locating behavior used by some species where males perch and wait for a female to pass by. Perching males go to certain places (such as hilltops) at certain times of the day (such as mornings). There they perch on plants or conspicuous objects like a stump or a boulder. Unmated females know where and when to rendezvous for a mate. Viceroys and Silver-spotted Skippers are perching species.

Proboscis   This is a drinking straw through which the butterfly draws up nectar, water, and other liquids. When not in use, the butterfly coils the proboscis and stores it under its head.

Puddling   This is the term for butterflies obtaining nutrients at damp earth. Puddling butterflies are usually freshly emerged males. Many butterflies in the following families puddle: Skippers, Swallowtails, Whites and Sulphurs, Gossamer Wings, and Snouts.

Roost   This is a quiet place to which butterflies retire for the night. They sometimes return to the same roost night after night. Butterflies also roost on cloudy or cool days.

Species   This is the term for all the individual butterflies that could, if brought together, mate readily and produce healthy, fertile offspring. All Monarchs, for example, are of the same species. In a butterfly's scientific name, the species name is easily recognized because it is always uncapitalized.

Walking Legs   This refers to the number of legs a butterfly uses for walking. All butterflies have six legs, but the forelegs of many butterflies, Brushfoots, for example, are shortened and not used for walking.

INDEX

Adelpha bredowii 114
Aglais milberti 94
Agraulis vanillae 74
Alfalfa Butterfly 46
American Painted Lady 96
Anaea andria 116
Anise Swallowtail 30, 96
Antennas 13, 20
  developing 98, 114, 116
  butterfly's false head 62
Ants 57
Anthocharis sara .44
Asterocampa celtis 118

Barred Yellow 52
Basilarchia archippus 110
Basilarchia arthemis 106
Basilarchia arthemis astyanax 108
Basilarchia lorquini 112
Basking 16, 20, 60, 64, 84, 102
Battus philenor .24
Bird Dropping Disguise 23
Black Swallowtail 28, 76
Brushfoots 79
Buckeye 50, 104

Cabbage Butterfly 42
California Sister .114

Caterpillar 126
  clinging ability 86
  coloring 28, 54
  eyesight 14
  hanging in "J" 92, 96
  false head 36
  group feeding 118
  leaf nest 16, 102
  legs 24
  molting 104
  molting to chrysalis 92, 116
  near molting 70, 74, 80
  osmeteria 23, 32
  poisonous 76
  pre-chrysalis .30
Celastrina argiolus 66
Cercyonis pegala 122
Chalcedon Checkerspot 86
Checkered Skipper 18
Checkered White 40
Chrysalis 34, 50, 92, 116
  butterfly about to emerge 98
  concealment .26
  gold decorations 128
  time in chrysalis 122
  transparent .98
Cleavage Lines 98
Cloudless Sulphur 46, 50

Cocoon 13
Colias eurytheme 46
Color Forms 46
Common Wood Nymph 122
Courtship 66
Crochets 86
Cryptic Coloration 28

Danaus gilippus 128
Danaus plexippus 126
Disruptive Coloration 112
Diversionary Tactics 62, 112, 122
Dog Face 48
Dung 23, 79, 88, 121

Eastern Tailed Blue 64
Egg(s) 108, 114, 118
  chain 88
  female searches for host 52
  mature in chrysalis 116
  strategy for laying many eggs 94
  wait period before laying 86
Epargyreus clarus .14
Epidemia helloides 60
Euphydryas chalcedona 86
Euptoieta claudia .80
Eurema daira 52
Eurema nicippe 54
Eurytides marcellus 26
Everes comyntas 64
Evolution 36

Eyesight, Butterfly 50, 84
Eyesight, Caterpillar 14

False Head
  butterfly 62
  caterpillar 36
Fiery Skipper 20
Flame Copper 58
Flash Coloration 104, 116
Foods, Non-floral 23, 69, 121
  dung 88
  fruit 90
  pollen 73, 76
Food Plant, See Host Plant
Fruit 90, 121

Genus 100
Giant Swallowtail 32, 112
Goatweed Butterfly 116
Gossamer Wings .57
Gray Hairstreak 62, 122
Great Spangled Fritillary 82
Gulf Fritillary 74

Hackberry Butterfly 50, 118
Heliconius charitonius 76
Heraclides aristodemus ponceanus 9
Heraclides cresphontes 32
Hibernation 88, 92, 94
Honeydew Glands 57
Hop Merchant 88, 90, 92

Host Plants 52, 62, 122
Hylephila phyleus 20

Juvenile Hormone 80
Junonia coenia 104

Leaf Nest 13, 16, 102
Legs-Caterpillar
    Clinging Ability 86
    True Legs-False Legs 24, 92
    Walking .13, 23, 39, 57, 69, 73, 79, 121, 125
Libytheana bachmanii 70
Life Span 28, 40, 58
    longest lived 92
    long lived 76
    shortest-lived 66
    winter/summer forms 52
Little Copper 58
Long-tailed Skipper 16
Longwings 73
Lorquin's Admiral 112
Lycaena phlaeas 58

Mate Location/Selection 84, 108
    wing pattern 14, 44
Mate Rejection 66
Mating 48, 52, 58, 66, 86
    color preference 46
Migration 54, 73, 88, 96
Mimicry 24, 36, 106, 110
Milbert's Tortoise Shell 94

Monarch 102, 108, 110, 116, 126, 128
Monarchs and Queens 125
Mourning Cloak 50, 92

Nectar 122
    spill avoidance 32
    sugar concentration 100
    used for energy 100
Nectar Flowers 122
    butterfly choice of 34, 82
Nettles, Stinging 102
Nymphalis antiopa 92

Osmeteria .23, 32
Overwintering (see also Hibernation) .52, 54, 96

Painted Lady 98, 102
Palpi 70
Papilio polyxenes 28
Papilio zelicaon 30
Patrolling 108
Pearl Crescent .84
Perching for females 84, 104, 108
Pheromones 30, 70
Phoebis sennae 50
Phyciodes tharos 84
Pieris rapae 42
Pipe-vine Swallowtail 24, 36, 106, 126
Poison 24, 76
    detoxifying .28
    in milkweed 126

mimicry .36, 106
   predators learn 128
Pollen 76
Polygonia comma 90
Polygonia interrogationis 88
Pontia protodice .40
Proboscis 20, 26, 42, 118
   developing 114, 116
   flower choice 82
   length 82, 90
   muscles in 74
   pollen 76
   puddling 106
Protective Coloration 94
Pterourus glaucus 34
Pterourus troilus .36
Puddling 102, 106
   for sperm maturation 114
   puddle club 64
Purplish Copper 60
Pyrgus communis 18

Queen 110, 116, 128
Question Mark 88, 92, 102

Red Admiral 102
Red-spotted Purple 24, 108
Roost 18, 42, 60

Sara Orange Tip 44
Satyrs, Browns, and Wood Nymphs 121

Scales 82
   hair-like .30
Schaus' Swallowtail 9, 112
Seasonal Forms 26, 52
Silver-spotted Skipper 14
Skippers 13
Sleepy Orange .54
Snake Disguise .36
Snouts 69
Snout Butterfly .70
Sperm 86
   mature in chrysalis 116
Speyeria cybele .82
Spicebush Swallowtail 24, 36
Spring Azure 66
Stretch Detectors 74
Strymon melinus 62
Swallowtails 23

Temperature Regulation (see also Basking) . . .102
Thistle 98
Tiger Swallowtail 32, 34, 108, 112
Toxin see Poison

Urbanus proteus 16

Vanessa annabella 100
Vanessa atalanta 102
Vanessa cardui .98
Vanessa virginiensis 96
Variegated Fritillary 80

Viceroy 110
Warning Coloration 73, 126
West Coast Lady .100
Western Parsley Swallowtail 30
Western Tailed Blue 64
White Admiral 106
Whites and Sulphurs 39
White/Yellow Color Forms 46
Wing(s) 20, 112
    anglewings 90
    closeup of 82
    in chrysalis 50, 116
    fluttering while feeding 32
    loss 62
    newly-emerged butterfly 112
    patterns, meaning 44
    protective coloration 94
    tailed hind wings 23, 62
    vibrating 102

Yellow/White Color Forms 46

Zebra .76, 112, 126
Zebra Swallowtail 26
Zerene cesonia 48

HOW TO USE RANGE MAPS

Year-round range

Migratory range

Areas highlighted in green are ranges where these butterflies can be found throughout the year.

Regions highlighted in yellow are ranges into which the particular butterfly may regularly and/or occasionally migrate.

A few maps show areas highlighted in orange. The orange highlights indicate a species that has a counterpart in another region. For example, the Eastern Tailed Blue on page 64 has a counterpart, the Western Tailed Blue. The region occupied by the Western Tailed Blue is highlighted in orange.